Worldwide
Wonders

NATURAL WONDERS

Clive Gifford

WAYLAND
www.waylandbooks.co.uk

First published in Great Britain in 2016 by Wayland

Editor: Nicola Edwards
Design: Peter Clayman

ISBN: 978 0 7502 9831 5
10 9 8 7 6 5 4 3 2 1

Wayland, an imprint of
Hachette Children's Group
Part of Hodder and Stoughton
Carmelite House
50 Victoria Embankment
London EC4Y 0DZ

An Hachette UK Company
www.hachette.co.uk
www.hachettechildrens.co.uk

Printed and bound in China

Picture acknowledgements: All images and graphic elements courtesy of Shutterstock
except p9b and 29b Corbis; p15t and br NASA; p25tr Wikimedia Commons.

Every attempt has been made to clear copyright. Should there be any
inadvertent omission, please apply to the publisher for rectification.

The website addresses (URLs) included in this book were valid at the time of
going to press. However, it is possible that contents or addresses may have
changed since the publication of this book. No responsibility for any such
changes can be accepted by either the author or the Publisher.

Contents

The Grand Canyon

This book is all about the world's most stunning natural wonders and there are few more striking than the Grand Canyon. Nearly five million people travel to the US state of Arizona each year to visit this majestic sight. Few are ever disappointed.

On a clear day, views of the canyon can stretch up to 160km into the distance.

Cutting the Canyon

Debate rages over when the canyon was formed, and estimates vary between 6 and 70 million years ago. The chief cause was the large, powerful and fast-flowing Colorado River. Stones, gravel and sediment carried along in the rushing water acted as a powerful abrasive, scouring and cutting the surrounding rocks. Over time, this giant winding canyon was formed. It measures 446km long and varies from around 160m to 29,000m in width. It has an average depth of 1.6km – more than four Empire State Buildings placed on top of each other!

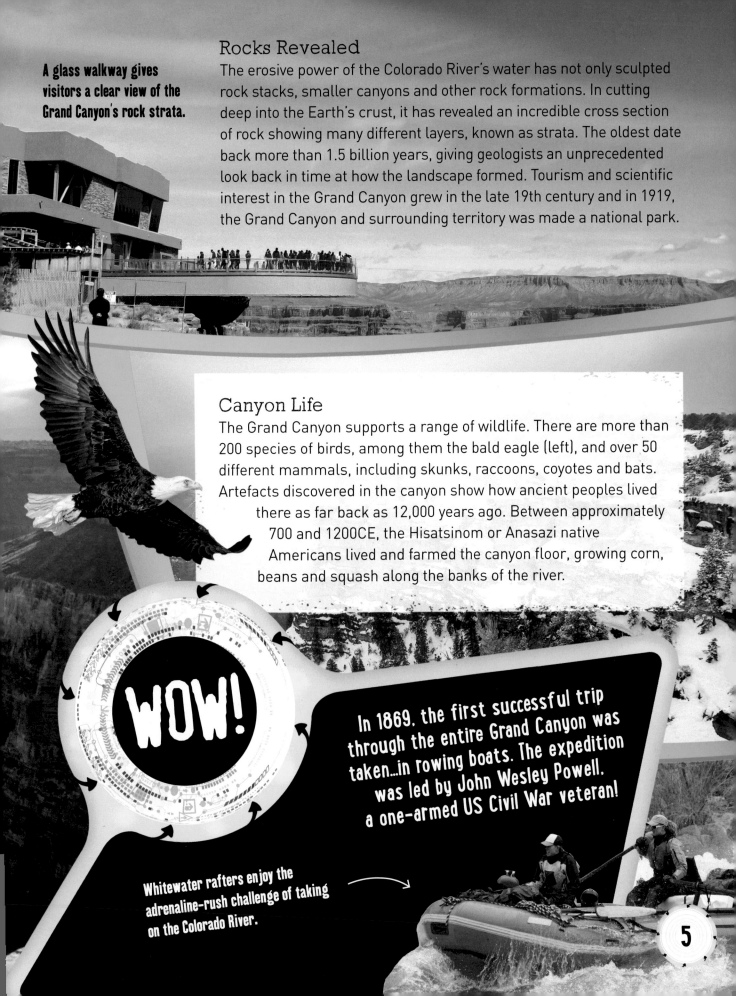

A glass walkway gives visitors a clear view of the Grand Canyon's rock strata.

Rocks Revealed

The erosive power of the Colorado River's water has not only sculpted rock stacks, smaller canyons and other rock formations. In cutting deep into the Earth's crust, it has revealed an incredible cross section of rock showing many different layers, known as strata. The oldest date back more than 1.5 billion years, giving geologists an unprecedented look back in time at how the landscape formed. Tourism and scientific interest in the Grand Canyon grew in the late 19th century and in 1919, the Grand Canyon and surrounding territory was made a national park.

Canyon Life

The Grand Canyon supports a range of wildlife. There are more than 200 species of birds, among them the bald eagle (left), and over 50 different mammals, including skunks, raccoons, coyotes and bats. Artefacts discovered in the canyon show how ancient peoples lived there as far back as 12,000 years ago. Between approximately 700 and 1200CE, the Hisatsinom or Anasazi native Americans lived and farmed the canyon floor, growing corn, beans and squash along the banks of the river.

WOW!

In 1869, the first successful trip through the entire Grand Canyon was taken...in rowing boats. The expedition was led by John Wesley Powell, a one-armed US Civil War veteran!

Whitewater rafters enjoy the adrenaline-rush challenge of taking on the Colorado River.

Victoria Falls

Deep in the heart of Africa lies an enormous wall of water: Victoria Falls. It is the worlds largest waterfall and one of the seven natural wonders of the world. Created by the 2,400km-long Zambezi River (the fourth largest in Africa). It flows from Zambia to Zimbabwe and empties into a series of narrow gorges.

The roaring noise made by the Falls can be heard 40km away.

Moonbows

During the wet season, from December to March, so much water thunders over the edge that a mist of water vapour can rise over 400m into the air. Locally, it is known as Mosi-os-Tunya meaning the 'smoke that thunders'. During this time, the spray from the falls can be seen nearly 50km away. At night, when there's a clear sky and a full Moon, a 'moonbow' (lunar rainbow) can form through the mist.

Deeper and deeper

Victoria Falls is not the highest falls (Angel Falls) or the widest (Khone Falls) but it has the longest, unbroken waterfall of water on Earth. The Falls were created by a fracture that occurred naturally in the basalt rock that lies under the area. This fracture caused a great crack in the Earth. This crack has formed these awe-inspiring Falls. The rock continues to erode as masses of water tumbles over the edge. The crack measures 108km deep in some places. The falling water crashing into the bottom of the falls is eroding the rocks all the time and making the drop deeper.

The level of water in the Falls reaches its peak in April, at the end of the rainy season.

Devil's Swimming Pool

Victoria Falls is 1,708 metres wide and 108 m high, more than twice as high as Niagara Falls. On average, around three million litres of water – that's 20,000 bath tubs full – flow over the Falls every second. During the dry season, from September to December, you can swim right by the edge of the Falls, in a naturally formed pool called the 'Devil's Swimming Pool'. The natural rock wall just below the water stops swimmers being washed over the edge.

WOW!

Diving into the 'Devil's Swimming Pool'

The falls attract extreme sport enthusiasts such as bungee jumpers, white-water rafters, and gorge-swingers looking for a free-fall adrenaline rush.

Sugarloaf Mountain

Big, bold and mostly bare of vegetation, Pão de Açúcar or Sugarloaf Mountain rises sharply upwards from the peninsula that juts out of Guanabara Bay in the booming Brazilian city of Rio de Janeiro. A Brazilian icon, many of the more than 1.5 million foreign tourists who visit Rio take a trip up the mountain to experience stunning views of the city below.

On the Bay

Guanabara Bay is found between the Botafogo district of Rio and the world-famous Copacabana beach. The bay forms a large, scenic natural harbour over which Sugarloaf Mountain looms. The 396m-high mountain, which is believed to be 600 million years old, was formed from tough granite and quartz that have resisted erosion far more than the surrounding rocks.

Viewed from Botafogo, Sugar Loaf Mountain towers over the rest of the peninsula.

What's in a Name?

The local Tamoios, native South Americans, called the mountain Pau-nh-açuquã, which means 'tall, pointy hill on its own', but Sugarloaf got its current name from Portuguese settlers and traders in the 16th and 17th centuries. At the time, sugar was extracted from cane as a liquid and poured into rounded cone-shaped moulds before being carried away by ships. The moulds looked much like the mountain, hence its name.

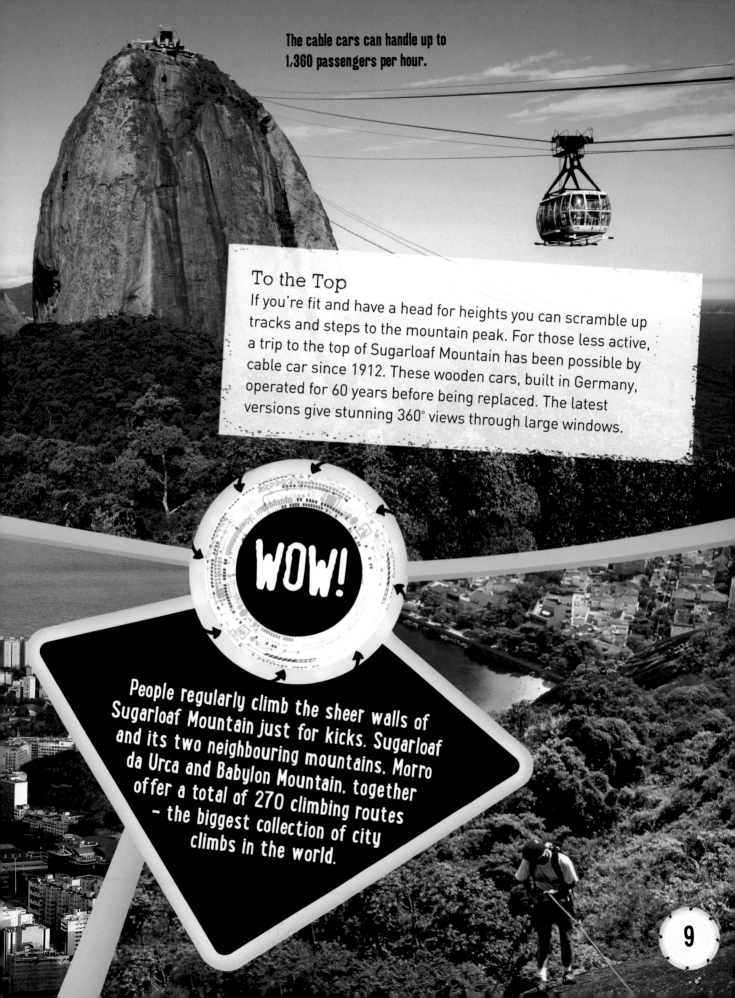

The cable cars can handle up to 1,360 passengers per hour.

To the Top

If you're fit and have a head for heights you can scramble up tracks and steps to the mountain peak. For those less active, a trip to the top of Sugarloaf Mountain has been possible by cable car since 1912. These wooden cars, built in Germany, operated for 60 years before being replaced. The latest versions give stunning 360° views through large windows.

WOW!

People regularly climb the sheer walls of Sugarloaf Mountain just for kicks. Sugarloaf and its two neighbouring mountains, Morro da Urca and Babylon Mountain, together offer a total of 270 climbing routes – the biggest collection of city climbs in the world.

The Great Barrier Reef

Barrier reefs are long, narrow formations of coral that lie mostly underwater parallel to the shore. Jam-packed with epic sea life, the Great Barrier Reef is the world's largest. It stretches for an incredible 2,300km close to the north-eastern coast of the Australian state of Queensland.

Crystal clear water reveals some of the reef structures when viewed from the air.

Coral Network

The Great Barrier Reef is a network of more than 2,000 smaller reefs along with tiny islands known as islets, sand bars and coral cays. Around 600 different species of coral, in all shapes, colours and sizes, are found in its waters.

It became a protected area, the Great Barrier Reef Marine Park in 1975 and spans an area of 344,400 km² – bigger than the UK, Switzerland and the Netherlands combined!

Reef Riches

The reefs are home to an extraordinarily rich array of marine life, including 3,000 species of mollusc, 133 types of sharks and rays and a staggering 1,625 species of fish. Sea turtles, many types of jellyfish and dolphins also inhabit its waters. In addition the reef attracts almost two million human visitors every year.

WOW!

You can send postcards with a special stamp from the Great Barrier Reef's only postbox which is situated 72km from shore on a floating dive platform in Agincourt Reef.

Under Threat

The Great Barrier Reef is a beautiful but fragile environment and it's vulnerable to a number of threats, from shipping damage and water pollution to rising sea temperatures caused by climate change. A rise in temperature affects and can kill the algae that the living coral relies on for food, causing coral to lose its vibrant colours (a phenomenon called coral bleaching) and, starved of nutrients, to die off.

Coral bleaching

Giant's Causeway

Northern Irelands most popular visitor attraction is a series of over 40,000 columns of volcanic rock forming geometric patterns on the rugged Antrim Coast.

Hot Rock

The Giant's Causeway was created some 60 million years ago as a result of volcanic activity. Molten basalt lava at a temperature of around 1,100°C was forced up through fissures (cracks) in the Earth's surface. It was cooled quickly by seawater to form thousands of mostly six-sided columns of basalt rock. Together, the columns form a pavement area along the North Sea coast.

The interlocking columns are buffeted by waves from the North Sea.

WOW!

According to Irish legend, the Causeway was built by the Irish giant Finn MacCool as a bridge across to the Scottish island of Staffa where he travelled to do battle with the Scottish giant, Benandonner.

Free to Enjoy

The Giant's Causeway became a UNESCO World Heritage Site in 1985 and remains free to visit. People can clamber all over the stones that form the pavement, although paths and viewpoints are roped off for safety. There's abundant seabird life to see, including fulmars, petrels, cormorants and razorbills, as well as the remains of a number of historic shipwrecks along the coast.

Visitors climb the hexagonal columns which form steps. A new visitors centre close to the site was opened in 2012. →

Tourists and Transport

As paintings and pamphlets about the extraordinary geological formations made them better known in the 18th and 19th centuries, so the numbers of visitors grew. In 1883, the world's first tram propelled by hydro-electric power began, carrying people from Portrush on a 14km route to the Causeway. The tram ceased operating in 1949, but since 2002, a narrow gauge railway service now carries 90 visitors at a time between the site and the town of Bushmills in carriages (below) pulled by a diesel or vintage steam train.

Aurora Borealis

Stunning and spectacular, epic patterns of light appear to dance across the night sky in the far northern regions of the planet. In 1619, the famous astronomer Galileo Galilei named the lights after Aurora, the Roman goddess of dawn and Boreas, the Greek god of the north wind. The aurora borealis is also commonly known as the northern lights.

Collisions with oxygen gas causes light green auroras.

Sent from the Sun

Aurora displays are created by tiny atomic particles, protons and electrons, streaming out from the Sun's surface. When they get close to the Earth, they collide high in the upper layers of the planet's atmosphere with gas molecules found there. These collisions mostly occur between 100 and 400km above the Earth's surface and give off light in a range of colours depending on the altitude of the collision and the gases involved. Light green tends to be the most common colour, but reds, pinks, oranges and blues can sometimes be seen too.

In the Zone

The stunning light displays are most commonly seen in an oval-shaped region surrounding the magnetic north pole. This area, known as the auroral zone, includes northern parts of Russia, Canada, Alaska and Scandinavia. At times, the lights can be seen further south in the UK and northern Europe.

North and South

A similar phenomenon occurs around the Magnetic South Pole. Known as the aurora australis or southern lights, this is mostly viewable in Antarctica and sometimes, in the southern parts of Australia, New Zealand and South America. In 2015, increased solar activity led to particularly spectacular southern lights in the skies observable from Tasmania, Sydney and other parts of Australia.

The lights are best viewed on clear nights from areas where there is no light pollution from big cities.

WOW!

Astronauts on board the International Space Station have an excellent view of the Northern Lights (below). The station's 400km orbit above Earth is around the same altitude as the highest aurora, so the astronauts can enjoy an unusual side-on view of the display.

Yellowstone Park

Founded in 1872 as America's first national park, Yellowstone's 8,983km² are a treasure trove of natural wonders.

Wyoming's Wonderland

Located mostly in the US state of Wyoming, Yellowstone Park is a mountain wilderness area with canyons, high hills, mineral-rich lakes, waterfalls and thick forests. The varying terrain provides a rich habitat for more than 150 bird species, as well as over 60 species of mammal, including elk, bison, black and grizzly bears, wolves and mountain lions.

Hot Spot

Yellowstone is positioned above a hot spot – a part of the Earth's crust where incredibly hot molten rock, called magma, is close to the surface. As a result, the park contains many vents where hot steam rises from below the Earth's surface as well as bubbling pools of hot mud and hot springs. The Grand Prismatic Spring is Yellowstone's and the United States' largest hot spring, measuring 112m in diameter and around 37m deep.

The bright colours around the fringes of the Grand Prismatic Spring are caused by different types of bacteria that thrive in its hot waters.

WOW!

More people are hurt by Yellowstone's herds of bison (above left) than by bears. Park regulations state that visitors must stay at least 23m away from bison and elk.

Forest Fires and Alien Invaders

Parks rangers in lookout towers check for forest fires caused by people or by lightning strikes before they blaze out of control. The park also has to deal with invasive species arriving in the park and damaging its ecosystem. The bark beetle, for example, has devastated thousands of Yellowstone's whitebark pine trees, the seeds of which are a crucial part of the diet diet of a grizzly bear (above).

A crowd watches an Old Faithful eruption of steam that typically lasts 2-5 minutes.

There She Blows!

Many of the more than 3.5 million people who visit Yellowstone every year come to see its hundreds of geysers. These hot springs contain water heated by magma below the Earth's surface. Pressure builds until water and steam are ejected violently from a vent in the ground. Yellowstone's Steamboat Geyser is its largest, firing water up to 90m into the air. Old Faithful is not as big but is more famous, due to the frequency and predictability of its eruptions. Every 35-120 minutes, this geyser spurts out up as many as 32,000l of boiling water to heights of up to 56m.

Serengeti Migration

Every year, several million hooved mammals make an extraordinary journey of more than 1,600km across the plains of Africa in search of fresh grazing land. Rush hour in the animal kingdom is rarely so busy as during the world's largest land mammal migration across Africa's Serengeti plain.

Travelling Together

Large numbers of grazing animals, such as gazelle, antelope, zebra and wildebeest, inhabit the Serengeti. This 30,000km² region of grassland and woodland occupies parts of two neighbouring countries, Kenya and Tanzania. The creatures move every year with the rains, heading towards new areas of lush plant growth that will give them the crucial minerals and water they need to survive.

The animals travel together for protection in large herds and smaller splinter herds. Each front hoof of a wildebeest leaves a trail of scent for others to follow.

Round Trip

Migration starts in the south-west Serengeti in Tanzania in late spring. The herds move north and then east, reaching the Masai Mara Game Reserve in Kenya between August and October. Continuing their journey, they follow the region's rains and plant growth on land, eventually returning to the south-western Serengeti between December and March.

Danger, Danger

Many of the migrating animals do not survive the trip; around 250,000 wildebeest, for example, die each year. The causes include starvation, exhaustion and attacks by a range of predators. Leopards, lightning-fast cheetahs, lions and hyenas may try to pick off young or weak members of a herd. River crossings can be particularly hazardous, with the threat of drowning and attacks by crocodiles.

Approximately 1.5 million wildebeest along with 360,000 gazelles and 200,000 zebra all make the trip.

WOW!

Between 400,000 and 500,000 baby wildebeest are born during the migration journey across the African plains.

A balloon flight offers stunning views of the plains.

Tourism and Threats

The Serengeti attracts large numbers of tourists who are keen to see Africa's big animals in their natural habitat. This brings in around US$1 billion of tourist revenues each year to Tanzania alone. However, threats to the region and its wildlife exist from poaching and deforestation, which has led to reduced water levels in rivers, and a scheme to build a large road right through the middle of the plain.

Uluru

Towering over the surrounding landscape in Australia's North West Territory, Uluru is a giant sandstone rock which has become one of the country's most iconic landmarks. Each year more than 250,000 tourists make the journey to central Australia, some braving high summer temperatures that can reach 47°C, to visit this awesome natural wonder.

Island Mountain

Uluru is an inselberg, an isolated mountain rising up from the surrounding plain. Even though most of its rock, some 2,500m, lies below the surface, Uluru still towers 348m over the land below. It's taller than the Eiffel Tower and over 3.5 times taller than Big Ben. The rock is approximately 3.6km long and 1.9km wide. Up close, it's clear to see how its surface has been shaped by wind and water erosion, forming gullies, shaped rocks and caves. Inside these caves are important rock paintings sacred to the local aboriginal people, the Anangu, who also gave Uluru its name.

From Sea to Ayers

Uluru is estimated to be more than 500 million years old and was once at the bottom of a sea. The tilting and folding of the Earth's crust thrust it upwards at an angle. Over millions of years the softer rocks were worn away to create the awesome sight that greets visitors today. Aboriginal peoples have lived in the region for some 30,000 years, but the first European to explore the inselberg was William Gosse in 1873. He named it Ayers Rock after the Chief Secretary of South Australia at the time, Sir Henry Ayers.

Uluru-Kata Tjuta National Park

In 1950, Uluru became the centre of a national park. Its land incorporated Kata Tjuta, also known as the Olgas, a similar rocky outcrop some 25km west of Uluru. Despite the hot, dry conditions in the Australian summer, around 400 plant species such as desert poplars, oak and acacia trees, survive in the park. There are also more than 150 animal species, ranging from types of birds, rodents and lizards to camels (below) and red kangaroos.

Anangu cave paintings describe traditional law and tell stories of their ancestors.

A walk around Uluru's base would clock up 9.4km.

WOW!

Uluru appears to change colour throughout the day, turning a particularly dark and vivid red at sunrise and sunset (below).

Niagara Falls

Forming part of the border between the US state of New York and the Canadian province of Ontario. Niagara Falls is a giant, scenic series of waterfalls that are breathtakingly beautiful. The crashing water attracts more than eight million visitors each year.

Niagara is derived from a native American iroquois word meaning 'the strait'.

Scour Power

Niagara Falls was formed via the receding and melting glaciers that covered much of North America during the last ice age and scoured out the basins of the continent's Great Lakes. The Niagara River flows between two of these Great Lakes, Lake Erie and Lake Ontario, on its way to the Atlantic Ocean. It has carved a deep gorge through the landscape and, by erosion, created three sets of falls. The American Falls and Bridal Falls are both located in US territory, while the majestic Horseshoe Falls lies mostly within Canada.

Constant Cascades

The curving Horseshoe Falls are incredibly broad – around 670m in width. Water cascades over these falls at a truly astonishing rate – as much as 2.4 million litres every single second. The water drops over 50m into the Niagara River below, making a thunderous noise and generating a thick mist as well as frequent rainbows.

Boats carry tourists up close to the spray-misted falls.

WOW!

The first person to survive travelling over the Horseshoe Falls in a barrel was 63-year-old ex-schoolteacher, Annie Edson Taylor in 1901.

Exploiting the Falls

The mighty falls have attracted interest and tourism for centuries – from honeymooners to high-wire walkers and other daredevils who've attempted to travel across or down the tumultuous water. Today, vast numbers of tourists come to view this natural wonder (right). Meanwhile, hydro-electric power plants on both sides of the river exploit the power of Niagara's running water to generate around 4.4 gigawatts of electricity, providing energy for more than two million homes.

Carlsbad Caverns National Park

Discovered over 100 years ago at the foot of New Mexico's Guadalupe Mountains. Carlsbad Caverns are an astonishing collection of caves, caverns and passageways decorated by staggeringly beautiful stalagmites, stalactites and other striking rock formations.

Giant stalagmites, including the Great Dome (right) abound in the caves.

Sea Story

About 250 million years ago, New Mexico was covered in a shallow sea ringed by a giant, horseshoe-shaped limestone reef. Over time, the sea drained and the reef was covered in sediment which turned into rock. This was then dissolved in places by strong sulphuric acid to form the caves and passageways. Dripping water containing sediment built up extraordinary cave features including the Giant Dome – a huge stalagmite 5m in diameter rising some 19m up from the cavern floor.

The spectacular Big Room is viewed from a visitor walkway.

WOW!

Found close to Carlsbad Cavern, Lechuguilla Cave was considered small and insignificant with passageways totalling less than 130m. In 1986, cave explorers began finding new passages and discovered the cave is, in fact, more than 222km long!

Massive Network

More than 200 caves and passageways make up the underground features of the Carlsbad Caverns. Over 190km of this cave network has been fully explored and mapped. The Big Room is the largest chamber in the caverns with an area of 33,210m² – about the size of 128 tennis courts!

Damage and Protection

In the past, the cave network was damaged by amateur explorers, speculators looking for treasure and guano miners who gathered bat droppings which were rich in minerals and made good fertiliser. Moves to protect the cave network began, and it became a national monument in 1923 and a national park seven years later. Today, access to the vast majority of the caves is limited to scientific expeditions in order to protect their delicate features.

The Dead Sea

The lowest body of water on Earth, the Dead Sea is a large, landlocked saltwater lake in the Jordan Rift Valley, bordered by Israel, Jordan and the West Bank. Its surface lies 429m below sea level. The Dead Sea area has its own microclimate, with low rainfall (usually less than 100mm per year) and consistently high temperatures between 20°C and 40°C.

Mineral Matters

Water flows into the Dead Sea primarily from the River Jordan but does not flow out. Instead, millions of litres of water evaporate into the atmosphere every day, leaving behind their impurities, often as mineral salt deposits. The water of the Dead Sea is almost nine times as salty as normal sea water. A litre of its water contains over 250g of mineral salts. This high salt concentration allows bathers to float with ease, but prevents all life except some bacteria from living in its waters.

Water from the Dead Sea evaporates leaving ridges of salt behind.

Shrinking Sea

In 1930, the Dead Sea was surveyed as having an area of 1,050km². In 2014, it was estimated to have shrunk to only 600km² and with a loss of 39m of depth. This is mostly due to more water being taken from the Jordan River for agriculture and industry before it enters the Dead Sea. In 2013, Israel, Jordan and Palestine signed a long-term agreement to build a 175km pipeline to carry water from the Red Sea over to the Dead Sea to help replenish its levels but critics fear it will not bring enough water to replace the large amount that evaporates from the sea.

WOW!

Asphalt (used today as a road covering) sometimes floats up in blocks from cracks in the bed of the Dead Sea. This was collected in Ancient Egyptian times and used to cover the outer surface of mummified bodies to stop water and insects getting in.

Salty Spa

The remarkable salty sea has been known and written about since ancient times. Aristotle, the ancient Greek philosopher, commented on the water's healing properties, and 2,000 years ago, Herod the Great established what may have been the first health resort close to its shores. Thousands of people travel to the Dead Sea today to enjoy its warm, dry climate, float in its mineral-rich waters and to spread the thick, black mud from the sea bed over their bodies (below) in the belief that the rich mineral deposits in the mud will benefit their skin.

More Natural Wonders

Natural wonders abound all over the planet in the form of mighty mountains, waterfalls and valleys as well as epic mass movements of creatures.

Roof of the World

At 8,848m above sea level, Mount Everest is the highest mountain in the world. Located in the mighty Himalaya mountain range, its peak was first climbed by New Zealand's Edmund Hillary and Nepal's Tenzing Norgay in 1953. Since then, more than 6,000 mountaineers have reached the summit. Potential conquerors of Everest have to pay large sums for permits to climb and must plan and train well for their ascent. Avalanches, falls, exhaustion and hypothermia take many lives on the hazardous climb to the summit.

Every year, climbers leave over 45 tonnes of rubbish on Everest, from broken equipment to discarded supplies and packaging. In 2014, Nepal's government set a new law making mountaineers each return from their climb with at least 8kg of waste.

Incredible Iguazu

This amazing waterfall, stretching almost 2,700m in a long curving arc, is found on the Iguazu River on the border of Brazil and Argentina. More than 1.5 million litres of water flow over the Iguazu Falls every second, giving rise to the name, which means 'Big Water' in the native South American Guarani language. National parks were established in Argentina (1934) and Brazil (1939) to conserve the rich natural life around the falls, including more than 400 bird and 2,000 plant species.

The waterfall has 275 separate drops, some as high as 82m.

Awesome Trench

Extending from Lebanon in the Middle East right the way through to Mozambique in south-eastern Africa, the Great Rift Valley system is a giant trench, almost 6,000km long. Scientists believe it was caused by two giant plates of Earth's crust moving apart creating a low-lying region in between. The Great Rift is home to much wildlife and is geologically active with volcanoes (above), hot springs and spouting geysers as well as dozens of lakes including the biggest and deepest lake in Africa, Lake Tanganyika which has a maximum depth of 1,470m.

Amazing migration

Christmas Island in the Indian Ocean is home to just 2,000 human inhabitants but over 30 million red crabs. Every year at the start of the wet season in October, the crabs migrate from the forests of the island to the coast to breed, turning the land red with their huge numbers.

Glossary and Further Information

altitude
The height of something, usually measured in metres or kilometres above sea level.

canyon
A deep gorge, often with a river running through it.

coral cays
Low-lying sandy islands on the surface of a coral reef.

erosion
The wearing away of surface rock and soil by wind, water and ice.

evaporate
When a liquid turns to vapour or gas, such as when heat from the Sun turns water in lakes and seas into water vapour in the air.

geologists
Scientists who study what the Earth is made of and how it formed.

geyser
A natural hot spring that occasionally sprays water and steam above the ground.

habitat
The home environment of a living thing.

hydro-electric power
Electricity that is generated by moving or falling water which turns devices called turbines that power an electricity generator.

hypothermia
A condition involving a serious drop in body temperature, often through exposure to a very cold environment.

iconic
Describes a very famous and instantly recognisable image or symbol of something.

inselberg
An isolated mountain rising up from the surrounding plain.

landlocked
Describes an area that is completely surrounded by land, rather than having a body of water as a boundary.

microclimate
Climatic conditions that are local to a small area and which differ from that of the surrounding areas.

migration
The regular movement of all or part of a bird or animal population from one area to another, for example in search of food or water, or to breed.

peninsula

An area of land that juts out from the main coast into the sea or lake so that it is surrounded on three sides by water.

sediment

A mass of material such as sand, mud and pieces of stone that settles to the bottom of a liquid.

stalactite

An icicle-like deposit formed from minerals in dripping water that hangs down from the roof of a cave.

stalagmite

A mound or column created by dripping water over long periods of time that grows upwards from the floor of a cave.

Books

Unpacked: Australia by Clive Gifford (Wayland, 2014)

Unpacked: Brazil by Susie Brooks (Wayland, 2016)

Visual Explorers: Wonders of the World by Paul Calver and Toby Reynolds (Franklin Watts, 2016)

Websites

http://www.westernriver.com/360/#prettyPhoto/0/
Travel through the Grand Canyon on a raft along the Colorado River and use your mouse or tablet controls to sweep round to watch the journey from any angle!

http://www.tothevictoriafalls.com/
Learn lots more about Victoria Falls and the Zambezi River at this highly informative website.

http://www.bbc.co.uk/programmes/b0198pww/clips
Watch lots of stunning clips about life in the Great Barrier Reef.

http://www.nps.gov/cave/learn/
photosmultimedia/photogallery.htm
Follow four photographic trails of different parts of Carlsbad Caverns.

http://www.nps.gov/yell/learn/nature/geysers.htm
Learn more about the geysers in Yellowstone Park and follow the links to predict how long it will take for Old Faithful to erupt.

http://www.eyesonafrica.net/migration.htm
See the movement of the herds of animals across the Serengeti month by month.

http://www.parksaustralia.gov.au/uluru/visual-journey.html
Take a visual journey around Uluru with this colourful photo gallery. Click on the links at the top to learn more about the local rock art and traditions.

Index

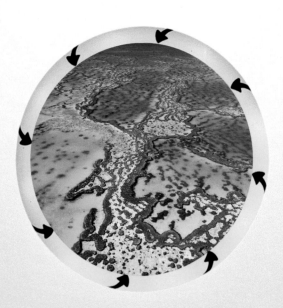